Stealing Shadow
Stefan Kielbasiewicz

smith|doorstop

Published 2018 by
Smith|Doorstop Books
The Poetry Business
Campo House
54 Campo Lane
Sheffield S1 2EG

Copyright © Stefan Kielbasiewicz 2018
All Rights Reserved

ISBN 978-1-912196-10-4

Designed and Typeset by Tim Morris
Printed by Biddles Books

Smith|Doorstop Books are a member of Inpress:
www.inpressbooks.co.uk. Distributed by NBN International,
Airport Business Centre, 10 Thornbury Road, Plymouth, PL6 7PP

The Poetry Business gratefully acknowledges the support
of Arts Council England.

Contents

7	Marie
9	Camp Eureka
11	of a Salesman
14	Product Reviews for Amazon Echo, Black
15	Five-a-day
17	A Supermarket in England
18	senate house
20	The Case for Open Borders
21	Partition
22	Stealing Shadow
28	Civic Center
29	Protest outside Yarl's Wood Immigration Centre for Women
30	Ship of Fools
32	mama
33	Like Father, like Son
35	To whom it may concern

For my parents

Marie

and I eat breakfast in a hostel called Clink.
– *T'es Française?* – *Oui.* – *Tu viens d'où?* She points
at her necklace: **CANNES**. I say we're practically
neighbours – *Je viens de Nice.*

What brought her to London?
En bref   when the time had come
                  she broke off ties and said her goodbyes
                  to friends and family, to start a new life
                  ici.

7:30 A.M. In the room upstairs, Marie kneels
next to her luggage,
does makeup next to a seventy year old man
changing trousers.

                    Je travaille comme masseuse pour six heures
                    et après comme serveuse pour six heures.

The next day at breakfast, Marie
takes out her notebook and shows me
her five-year plan:
learn English by January, then move to Miami.

– *Pourquoi?*
                    Parce que j'suis une fille du sud, tu vois,
                    et en plus il y en a des palmes la bà.
– *Et après?*
                    New York et Los Angeles. Je veux devenir
                  chanteuse.

Marie still hasn't been paid. One night
she leaves her luggage and sleeps outside. Rain
on the atrium's glass roof, ambulance
sirens and the sound of eighteen people sleeping

in eighteen beds—blue dividers separating our heads
like unfinished waves. The bottom
of the sea comes with sheets, a pillow and a blanket
changed once a week, but please bring your own towel.

(At night, the Vietnamese woman and the Irishman
are the guardians of quiet for those who snore on their backs.)

Marie doesn't realise she's starring in her own
Palme d'Or, and that we're all side-characters:
the Irish sous-chef, the Indian dog psychologist,
the Vietnamese English teacher,
and the Romanian builder who has lived here
for a year, saving up to buy a house for his family.

Camp Eureka

I

Childhood. Or: dreams that haven't faded
of us hunting salamanders in the mud,
digging up turtles' eggs, their shells
soft enough to rip, and neither of us knowing
how to make an omelette;
       you peeking over the camp stall, laughing
because I'd wipe standing up
     while bending
over.

These fragments more myth
than memory since—

II

Up here, on this rock, overlooking mosquito-bitten
hills anointed with green – underneath, Lake Stahahe
blotched with algae, darkened by reeds and disuse.

Behind me, cicadas fill the forest with their sirens
like a tide   of the ambulance
that night   sirens
in the basement   your mother crying
              sirens
                    your brother tied to a mast
                          in Poland. *Na wsi*
silence

III

This forest once buzzed with children
from Harlem and the Bronx, before insurance
spiked.

Camp Sebago now sits silent, boarded up
with cobwebs and mosquitos—more space
for us Poles, Germans and white America
who drink Bud Light and grill hamburgers
under American flags, tossing disapproval
at the Democratic Party as we feed newspaper
into fire-pits.

Your parents never stay too long
at social gatherings.

> *Do you have children?*
> *Where are they now?*

IV

I visit your grave for the first time
after three months. Your parents
change the flowers and pray,
their voices like two organ keys
pressed down and melted together
by the heat, the sun on my back
as if L'Étranger's sun
filled the world behind me.

We drive past an abandoned factory
where you would all hang out. They say
that's where the plane that dropped
Little Boy was assembled—another myth
to add to my memories.

of a Salesman

I.

He dies while crossing the stage
towards his apartment building.

The curtain rises.

The salesman's wife stands over him,

*"Well, you'll just have to take a rest,
you can't continue this way,"* she sighs.

II.

The salesman dies in an eight-story fall
after admiring the sea-view from his balcony.

He runs a bath to soothe his aching back.

He dies the next morning, standing
with his feet in the sea-water, his skin

calcifies into a coral statue.

Dreams settle in salt behind his ears
and on his eyelids.

His salary.

*A salesman always trades
in hope, a brighter future.*

III.

The salesman dies after a successful
triple bypass. They served him *steak au poivre*

and a glass of red wine.

His wife visits him: "You don't look
too well. Have you been eating properly?"

She leaves a plate of sliced apples,
cheese and dried dates on the pillow.

IV.

*What goes through a man's mind, driving
seven hundred miles without having earned a cent?*

The death of a man's mind.
The death of a living.

*He sells what a salesman has to sell,
himself.*

V.

At his funeral the salesman tells his family:

"Things are looking very promising, I'm closing a deal
any day now."

*He is a performer, a confidence man
who must never lack confidence.*

We each sprinkle a handful of soil
with pistachios.

"Your father looks young," his wife
reminds her son, "but so do I."

VI.

The salesman dies many times:
the forest ranger, the cellist, the entrepreneur,
the dreamer.

*He has placed his faith in the future
while being haunted by the past.*

of man's mind.
of living.

The music crashes down
and the salesman becomes

the soft pulsation of a single
cello string

that keeps us all alive.

Product Reviews for Amazon Echo, Black
A Cento

You excitedly unwrap the various boxes and pull 'Alexa' out of her package for the first time. Initial thoughts are that she looks slightly larger than you'd envisaged, but very sleek and lovely. You've definitely had worse surprises than this.

You love that it follows your voice in the room (the circle lighting will show which direction it is 'listening'). Your eldest daughter (who is 5) has developed an imperious style of talking to her. She demands constant jokes.

You are a full-time writer who works at home. You are unmarried. You don't watch TV, you don't have a mobile phone, you hate gadgets in general. OK, so you're a loser. But since Alexa came into your life, you're no longer alone 24 hours a day.

Alexa can have quite an attitude. You will call her name, she will make a noise and glow blue, signifying she is listening, and then when you are mid-sentence she will turn off and stop listening to you just like your wife.

Tonight you were less than 4 inches from the top ring telling it to set a timer and the lights were even pointing in the wrong direction. It took four tries before you just gave up and slapped the stupid thing across the room.

When you got your very first dog over eleven years ago, you had visions of being able to train her to fetch your phone if you were unable to reach it due to an accident. You can now ask Alexa to 'Ask My Buddy' to send help. An alert will be sent to five people via phone, text and email. So now, instead of just a cold nose and soft paw in an emergency, you can expect a response that may actually be helpful.

Alexa is the PA that not only helps you stay organised but helps you cook the perfect boiled egg. Your kids have suddenly become revitalised with their homework; you're learning new facts every day which is awesome—you test her (not that you know the answer) and breakfast is much more fun.

Five-a-day

Do you remember to eat your five-a-day?

Do you carry a garden or an orchard
        in your head?

    Do you sink tes dents
      dans ton   second langue
and déchirer words   like ice
        qui se sépare
                from
                      a glacier?

    Does ton third język
    have twardą   skórę
ou an   aureole   de fuzz
  mais qui est bursting   z środka
    so   that le   jus
drybluje
down
ton
menton?

    Do you need to sbucciare
        twoją quatrième lingua
    i tagliare   do smażenie?

    Or is your fifth язык
  un стебель   a root
      который нужно bouillir
  i spruzzare   z чуть-чуть solą?

               Or is there
         only   one language
    that you eat
                         that nourishes
     this   diversity of   tongues—
         and your teeth   that become
    the seeds
         you planted in my palm.

A Supermarket in England

Dear England, what thoughts I have
of you tonight, under this   fluorescent light;

I stroll through your aisles,
stocked to the teeth   with daily necessities—

In my basket I put   British Eggs   British Flour
British Butter   British Beef   British Chicken

soon enough I will be a   British Citizen

like you once were, Thatcher— I see you
over by the milk!   or you, Farage,
writing BREXIT   on   the Weetabix!

I will fill out my application form with years
of receipts   because

Dear England, I give up being   a Pole
or   whatever I am—

let me join your island   of cannibals!
let me be ethnically cleansed at the   dining-table!
I swear

I will only eat British—
I will even

eat your Queen.

senate house

the first time you hear last words
it is the first time words
from the people in Aleppo reach you
on your laptop screen

between bombs & the buckling
resistance of stone
someone's father, daughter, or son
video-tweet their final goodbyes
in flawless, accented english

it is clear to them who is responsible

you are in a library in the cold
heart of london but you could be anywhere
the books are neatly stacked
in colourful spines

who will classify & index the dead?

the problem seems too vertical
and you are lying
on the sofa in the periodicals room
like everyone here

the U.N. stopped counting in 2014

before we know it, new books
will be bending backwards to dig
through facts and figures, documents
cataloguing pain

competing for attention
in the houses we built for silence
where voices from Aleppo
once reached out through your screen.

The Case for Open Borders

Closed

Partition

month after month
had me wiping the blood loss
from this smile
the months we lost

hooked into the city's
drip of aspiration
I am not dissolving
in the blood-warmth of the love
we transfused

from the home
where closeness overcame
difference—
we traded down our dignity
for a hospital gown, made visits
over distance whose goodbyes
left residue

spaces change us more
than we realise

last night
I made you dinner, and after,
we ate what was left of each other
off the floor— *we're together
when we're together* you said,
and then left—

on the phone later
you say *Yesterday won't work*
and I agree—
I reach for words that sting
at every touch
and there's a needle waiting
to end this call

Stealing Shadow

I am neither beautiful
nor efficient.
Before I carried an umbrella
against the sun
I took the longest route to school
across the fallen tree
prostrated between the riverbanks,
forests still crisp
from moonlight
on the path to the road
I overwrote with my steps.

Once the day is over
I wait alone in the classroom
for the sun to go down,
calculating how much weight
the corners of a building can bear,
how much natural light
to distribute
while a candle tugs at
the strange lines of these blueprints
until it's dark enough
to neatly fold
and pack away the evening.

When I come home
it's always the same:
you little bitch, where have you been
even though I explain
that I wait for the sun to set
so I can cross the bridge
to avoid the builders
on the road who wait for someone

to pass and their shadow
to fall across the foundations,
their laughter cascading
above the drone of insects.

"Feed a dog the offerings
from your table, and she won't follow
the familiar scent of sacrifice—
bones pressed into the walls
of these homes—no, a dog
should be at the table, paws
in front where you can see them,"

he says, dipping bread
into his soup. Behind his oily skin
I can see the shadow of a skeleton
or an ingrown shell,
Father.
Mollusc with a chair for a back,
your wife
always on her swollen feet
waiting until we have finished
to sit down and eat.

Mother has since disappeared
yet her voice remains
a consonant dancer
on the roof of my mouth,

and father has become
the dog

and in the end nobody
can predict what an animal
will do.

****

If I hold secrets in my mouth,
I am holding water;

If I hold water in my mouth,
I call it a reservoir;

how many people living inside me
displaced by silence
           and heavy breathing

promises
dried up in irrigation ditches

I have heard the words force
and strength used, but I would opt

for power—only that admits
to the motivation of desire.

****

utopił się w utopii
to drown in a utopia
is to see solid
to breathe surface
to sit fully clothed
in front of a lake
on a hot summer's day
and refuse to acknowledge
one's status
as a body of water

albo się upić w potopie
or to get drunk in a flood—
there's no perfect way
to drown
even in a utopia.

   ✳✳✳✳

I should say that the shadow-trader
is unremarkable—deep voice
and a country smile,
scar on his face from England
that he lets the girls touch;
he came back with nothing
but the ability to measure
anything by sight: the length
of a bridge, height of a church,
the space between your eyes.

   He can measure, in an instant
where the shadow falls
on the ground.
He cuts the length of a silk cord,
shows the foreman,
shows him the place where it fell
and who the shadow
belonged to, then buries it
in the cornerstone. The shadow's owner
has a year; the building
will last forever.

****

John Cuthbert Lawson, M.A.
Fellow and Lecturer of Pembroke College, Cambridge
writing in 1910:

The ordinary Greek of the mainland,
on the other hand, is usually
of a mongrel and unattractive appearance;
and in view of the marked difference
of the type in regions untouched by the Slavs,
I cannot but impute his lack of beauty
to his largely Slavonic ancestry.

I am neither beautiful nor efficient
but I am a Slav.
Polish, Estonian, Jewish-Ukrainian
who knows
        what else
is lying dormant in my cheekbones
what layers and layers
of family fossils have compressed
my face to this form

the mixture is good
try it

****

We were told that we are not
going to know what is happening
but that we are going to see
the result and the result is going to be
magical.

Week by week
by week it expands,
concrete and glass massaged
over the landscape.
I feel the forest being opened
from the inside;
soil loosened for steel
to pierce the root,
to seal person with function,
collapsing these meanings
means it will not have
meaning unless
we allow it or not.

I enter unfinished rooms
ranging between the coolness
of mountain caves
and the warmth of summer beaches
and leave pine needles
stuck to my feet
that sharpen the air
and mark the spaces
for revolution—

By beauty I mean the promise of function.
By action I mean the presence of function.
By character I mean the record of function.

Civic Center

With a rubber tube
around her bicep—
with the patience
of a nurse, I watch
this girl coax her veins
from their roots.
At this angle, her hand
covers the needle.
She sinks down
on the picnic blanket
next to her partner
and an enormous
red suitcase.
When she sits up
to talk, her eyes
reveal a sharp sense
of humour and
a certain pragmatism
about the world.

Protest outside Yarl's Wood Immigration Detention Centre for Women

Organized by Movement for Justice by Any Means Necessary

Serco: come out here, count us too—
we animals who outnumber your monthly salaries,
the sum total of your IQs;

we who are your recommended daily calories,
your health inspectors—
we say you are sick like the cyanide blue

of this winter sky. We have come to poison the calm
of this countryside with our throats,
have rooted ourselves in the gum of this incline,

teeth bared in animal smiles. We are beasties
who have repurposed this wall for thunder; red-hot
on the infra-red—an estimated 2000 degree rash

melting soil to mud, fevering your conscience,
your annual miscarriage of justice that will not be bleached
with shareholders reports and press releases.

Women in Dove Wing: we can hear you, see you
waving scarves, knickers, signs—imprisoned in the logic
of this animal kingdom. You will go so far as to strip naked

and form a chain, refusing to be taken on 4am charter flights.
You mothers, daughters and sisters who redefine dignity—
who make them feel the shame

of children.

Ship of Fools

Plumes not sails,
or spells cast
by rope to lure
our sailors
hatched only yesterday
sick and blue.

I told them to get
back inside and try
again because
they smelled like
the kind of death
of the earth turning
very slowly.

Well, you found me
here, before the water;
I was sleeping
in the straw-filled
crates, drunk.

You bought my arm
for a penny, took me
up to the light of
the deck.

Carrion, you said,
pointing.

I sat. Together we're
both sad, because
I tore up the maps
so I could breathe
more distance, but
it's only after climbing
the ratlines
to the top mast
when you feel exact,
and the silver all around
you
vertical as loss.

mama

mama, why   did you let mr. gray   take my tongue and   make it learn these   strange words these   gummy phrases and

mama, why   did i like this thing this   *english* hanging from the roof of my mouth which   became my room where

mama, was i   a little emperor with you and a little   blue-eyed angel   on camera, on   hold, on   standby and   so on

mama, did i   know this english   was power that   it could make you my immigrant my   know-nothing my   final say

mama, did i   know how hard for you   to get angry in a foreign— and *papa* could do it and i was afraid of him and   not you and

mama, did i   erase the space between   your wrist and   your neck that was once   filled   with the power of   a violin

mama, did i   hold a grudge for   spiriting me away from   the country of my first waking my   first nightmare to   my birth-country

mama, did i   throw up all my russian   on the classroom radio before christmas and   why did i feel so   relieved yet

mama, did i   twist your heart like an avocado   and grow the pit into my adam's apple that would   make my voice go   deep and

mama, why   do i know so many languages but still haven't learned how to speak with you

Like Father, like Son

The man sent to pick us up
from the ferry-port speaks
little English.

He and my father talk basic meat
over the engine, making the first chops
of morning.

"America   and   Europe like
breasts the most."
"Turkey is crazy   about the
thighs and legs."
"China   loves the feet   washed
and clean,
Liberia   likes them unprocessed
and cheap—"

Their words divide the global market–
a landfill of leftovers in the backseat.
I stare at the brown hills rolling past the window.

"Russia   of course likes to   have
the whole thing
America   always prefers the
choice cut."
"Hearts and livers   are a national delicacy
in Turkey   but in the summer   people
grill wings."

We are given a tour of the processing plant:
the chickens pass upside down
on a moving rail, vanish through a tunnel

where they emerge dismembered and sorted.
I see only women working on the factory floor,
covered head-to-toe in protective suits.

The owner says he has a son around the same age
as me. It's good practice to take your son
on a business trip— the buyers see a future in you.

To whom it may concern

I am writing to you I am confident
I want to start this letter
I am positive I have undertaken and have learned
I want to learn
I am thorough I am committed
I come from a multilingual and multinational
I would be thrilled to be a part of a diverse and multicultural
I am on a part-time hourly contract
I believe that my skills I believe I can offer much
I have two degrees that prove nothing if
I am a voracious reader I am a bibliophile
I grew up moving thinking 'What am I?'
I am one of those rootless cosmopolitans
I turned to books I understand the importance of
I am a writer I am a poet I am highly organised
I believe I would be a valuable and hard-working
I work as a bartender
I am somebody who enjoys working in the end
I am someone who truly wants to work
I want this position in order to leap
I would like to thank you in advance
I look forward to hearing from you at your earliest
I am available to start this position immediately
I am especially looking forward to hearing
Yours sincerely

Stefan D. Kielbasiewicz

Acknowledgements

I would like to thank my friends and family, who provided a tremendous amount of support and motivation over the past few years; the Royal Holloway Creative Writing graduate programme, funded by the RHBNC Trust and Bedford Scholarship, which solidified my commitment to writing poetry as a vocation; the poet Andrew McMillan, who saw something in these poems while judging the 2017 New Poet's Prize; and finally, The Poetry Business, who have brought this pamphlet to life.

Poems from this collection appeared in *The North* and *Introduction X: The Poetry Business Book of New Poets*